BASSMASTER

SPINNERBAIT BASSIN'

100 Tips for Using Spinnerbaits

A How-To Book From BASSMASTER® Magazine

Edited By
Wade Bourne And The Staff
Of BASSMASTER® Magazine

ILLUSTRATIONS BY
Marilyn Heard

COVER PHOTO BY
Ed Mendus

COVER DESIGN BY
Jeffrey K. Preg

A HOW-TO BOOK FROM B.A.S.S.®

Second Edition, 1994
PUBLISHER, **Helen Sevier**
EDITOR, **Dave Ellison**
EXECUTIVE ART DIRECTOR, **Glo Fomby**
ART DIRECTOR, **Rebecca Hockman-Carlisle**

Copyright 1994 by B.A.S.S., Inc.
5845 Carmichael Road
Montgomery, Alabama 36117

Manufactured in the United States of America

PREFACE

The spinnerbait is one of the most versatile lures in the world of bass fishing. Spinnerbaits come in a wide array of sizes, colors, and configurations. They can be used in a diverse number of places and with a variety of techniques. Spinnerbaits are effective in shallow water, deep water, muddy water, clear water; in heavy cover, open flats; during early morning, noon, and night. If there's a bass willing to bite, there's a spinnerbait and a technique that will take him.

Following is a collection of wisdom on how to use these lures. For easy reference, the tips are divided into four separate categories covering these topics:

Category I — **Choosing The Right Spinnerbaits.** Tips here tell you which baits to select for specific fishing circumstances. Variables to consider in making your choice include lure size, color, blade configuration, and blade type.

Category II — **Where To Fish Spinnerbaits.** This section describes likely places to cast spinnerbaits and the right techniques for working them.

Category III — **Spinnerbait Tips And Tackle.** This section provides advice on general techniques for more efficient spinnerbait use — ideas that can be applied in a broad range of circumstances. It also includes proper choice of tackle for using spinnerbaits.

Category IV — **Altering Spinnerbaits.** This section covers how to alter spinnerbaits if a lure doesn't meet a particular fishing situation. Sometimes making just slight changes in a bait can result in dramatic bass-catching rewards.

Because of their similarity to spinnerbaits, buzzbait tips also are included in this book. Together, these two lure types comprise a deadly arsenal to use on bass. It's a simple fact that the angler who masters these baits will catch more fish and have more fun on the water. So learn and enjoy!

Wade Bourne

CONTENTS

. . . .

Part I
Choosing The Right Spinnerbait

5

Part II
Where To Fish Spinnerbaits

Part III
Spinnerbait Tips And Tackle

Part IV
Altering Spinnerbaits

I

CHOOSING THE RIGHT SPINNERBAIT

Select Spinnerbait Weight According to Water Depth

Spinnerbaits are commonly bought in three sizes: 3/16 oz., 1/4 oz., and 1/2 oz. A simple rule of thumb in deciding which baits to buy and use is: Use lighter baits for shallower water and heavier baits for deeper water. The 3/16-oz. class of spinnerbaits should be fished in 0-4 feet of water; 1/4-oz. lures in 4-8 feet of water; and 1/2 oz. deeper than 8 feet.

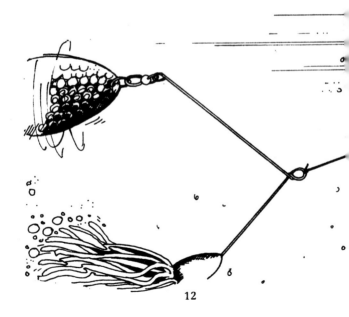

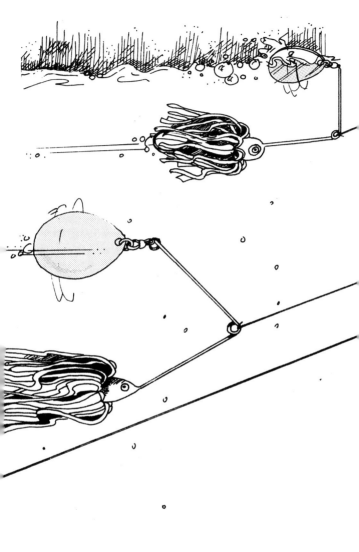

13

Buy Spinnerbaits With Good Swivels

One mark of a spinnerbait's quality is the type of swivel used to connect its blade. The best baits have ball-bearing swivels, rather than the more common crane swivel. Baits with ball-bearing swivels cost more because these swivels are made from stainless steel.

Bass anglers should purchase the better-quality baits if they can afford them because the blades turn more freely on the ball-bearing swivels. This means better blade vibration when the lure is worked deeper and/or slower. When these vibrations are steady, it's easier for anglers to detect subtle changes in the vibration pattern, which translate into soft strikes.

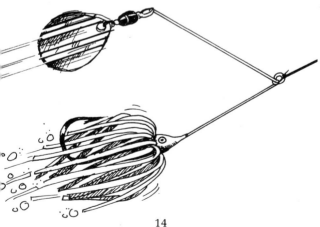

Use Willow-Leaf Spinner When Working Current

Working spinnerbaits in current may present problems if the current is strong and/or the baits' blades are the popular Colorado (oval) variety. In such a situation, try a spinnerbait with a willow-leaf (elongated) blade, or replace the Colorado blade on your original bait with a willow leaf. Its elongated blade and tight rotation create less resistance during retrieve, making the bait easier to feel and control.

Select Single Or Tandem Spinnerbaits According To Water Depth

S ome spinners have one blade; others have two — called "tandem spinners." Single-bladed baits are generally used for fishing in deeper water when slower retrieves are the rule. Tandem-bladed spinners are designed for use close to the surface. Two blades churning (as opposed to one) give the lure more buoyancy and hold it up easier.

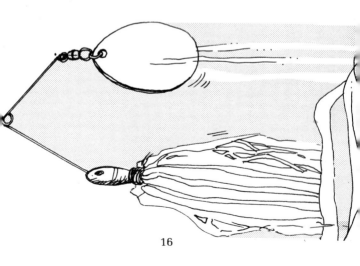

Observe Water Clarity To Determine Spinnerbait Color

Expert bass anglers choose spinnerbait colors to match the condition and color of the water they intend to fish. For example, if the water is muddy or heavily stained, use baits with chartreuse, yellow, lime-green, or brown and orange skirts. In clear water use white, blue, or green. At night when the moon is bright, cast darker colors, such as black, brown, or purple.

Match Arm Length To Cover Being Fished

The length of a spinnerbait's arm — the wire to which the blade is attached — is the main determinant to how weedless a particular bait will be. Baits with long arms are more weedless; those with short arms are less weedless. It's important, then, to match bait selection with the amount and type of cover you're fishing. In heavy cover, use a long-armed bait. When cover is sparse, it's better to select a spinnerbait with a short arm. The reason for not using a long-armed bait in both circumstances is that the percentage of hookups per strikes is generally higher with short-armed baits.

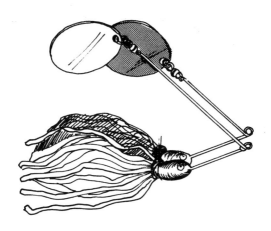

Fish Maxi-Spinner For Trophy Bass

O ne new trend in spinnerbait fishing is the use of huge baits when seeking trophy bass. Many pros are now fishing with spinnerbaits weighing 1 ounce, as opposed to standard spinnerbait sizes of 1/4 or 3/8 oz. These lures sport blades as large as the top of a baby-food jar. Such blades displace much more water and create stronger vibrations during retrieve, two characteristics which many anglers feel attract bigger bass.

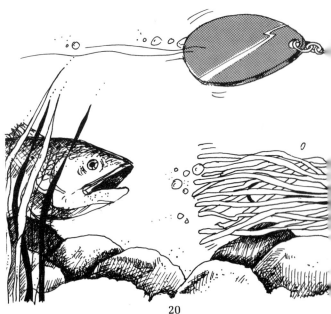

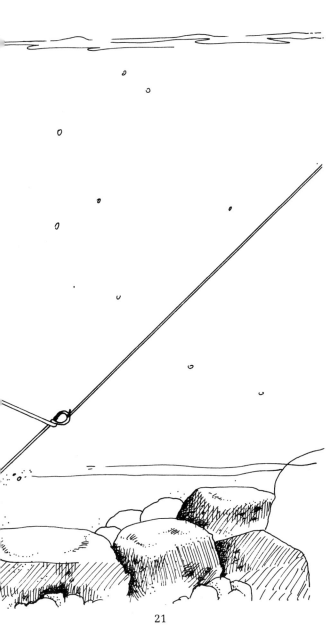

Select Spinnerbait With Weedguard For Fishing Heavy Cover

S pinnerbaits, especially those with long arms are fairly weedless by design. Yet there may be times when anglers casting into extremely heavy cover need extra protection from snagging. To gain such an advantage, use a spinnerbait with a plastic-bristle weedguard; this guards the hook against hang ups. When a bass clamps down and the angler strikes back, however, the weedguard gives way and allows the hook to penetrate the fish's jaw.

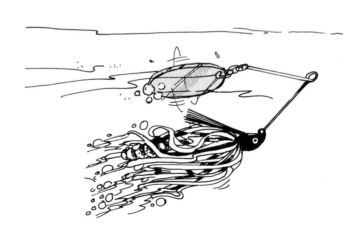

Use Planing-Head Spinnerbaits
For Stubborn Bass

When bass are holed up in cover and reluctant to hit, slowing your spinnerbait — keeping it in the strike zone longer — is crucial. Slow-moving lures generally produce better on inactive bass.

One type lure that can be worked at a very slow rate is the planing-head spinnerbait. Instead of a regular molded-lead head, the planing-head spinner has a flattened, lightweight metal head. This lack of weight and gullwing design gives the bait a buoyance which allows it to be retrieved at slower speeds without sinking to the bottom.

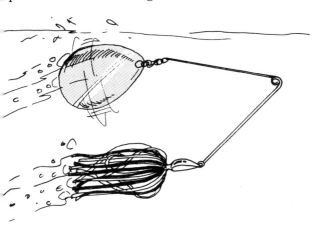

Use Clear Plastic Blade In Clear Water

S ometimes bass are jittery in extremely clear water, wary of the flash of a metal-bladed spinnerbait. In such a circumstance, try a bait with a clear-plastic blade. The vibration and sound are still there to attract fish, but the bright flash of the metallic blade is eliminated.

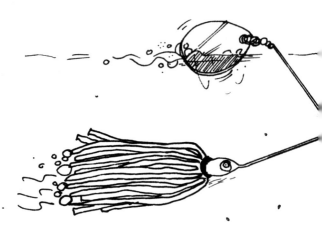

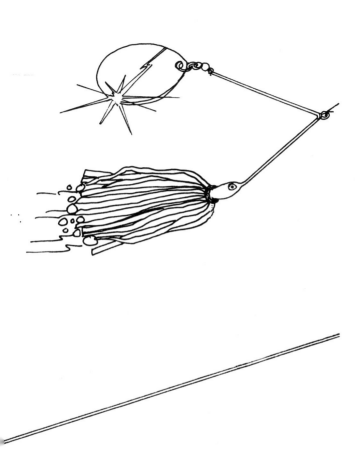

11 *tip*

For Night Fishing, Let Moonlight Determine Spinnerbait Color

When night fishing with spinnerbaits, rely on moonlight conditions to help you select the color lure to use.

During a full moon, for example, choose a bait with a light-colored skirt such as green and white, and add a similar-colored pork chunk. During a dark moon, opt for purple in combination with other dark colors such as purple and brown skirt and purple pork frog. Over the years, purple has proved to be an extremely effective night-fishing color.

Fish Spinner/Minnow Combination

S pinners are excellent bass lures, and so are live minnows. Team these two, and you have a dynamite combination.

The proper spinner to use is an in-line variety: a small blade with a piece of wire at either end. On one end is a snap to attach the hook; on the other, a loop to tie the line. Retrieve this bait very slowly. The flash of the blade and the struggling minnow are a very appealing, exciting combination to curious fish.

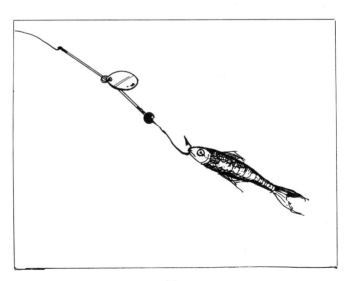

Work Spinnerbait
Down-Current, Along Eddy Edges

In a steady current in a river or lake, bass hold in eddy pockets, behind logs and rocks, facing upstream to watch for food washing by. In this situation, position yourself downstream from the eddy. Cast a spinnerbait upstream and retrieve it back with the current, right along the edge of the eddy. The strikes should come right at the head of where the current breaks around the cover.

Choose Proper Spinnerbait
For Clear Water

Fishing standard spinnerbaits in extremely clear water often will spook bass. But using lures specifically designed for this condition can produce amazing results. Clear-water spinnerbaits are small in size. They have clear Lexan (hard plastic) blades, and grubtails are added as trailers. These baits should be fished fast and close to the surface.

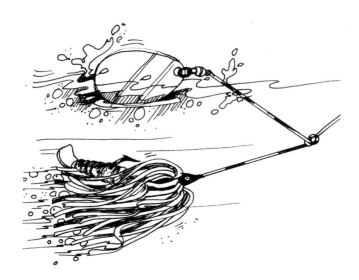

Match Spinnerbait Size To That Of Natural Food

When choosing a spinnerbait, keep in mind the size of baitfish or food on which the bass are feeding. Following a baitfish hatch, when the main food source is tiny fry, small baits with diminutive blades may produce more action than standard-sized baits.

Pump Spinnerbait Down
Rocky Bluffs, Riprap

Spinnerbaits worked with a lift-and-drop technique are extremely effective along rocky bluffs and riprap banks. Cast the bait — a short-armed spinnerbait, possibly in front of a #11 pork chunk trailer — perpendicular to the bank, close to the shoreline, and allow it to sink to the bottom. Then lift the bait with your rod tip, move it forward a short distance, and allow it to flutter back to the bottom on a tight line, then repeat the procedure until the lure is past the structure. Strikes generally occur as the bait is falling.

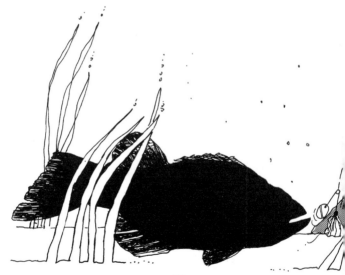

Try Jumbo Spinnerbait
For Night Fishing

When standard-sized spinnerbaits fail to produce bass while night fishing, try a jumbo, 1-oz. model. This large bait sets up a hard-thumping action that sometimes provokes otherwise tight-mouthed fish to bite. Fish such a bait in deep water, 15-30 feet, and use a very slow retrieve.

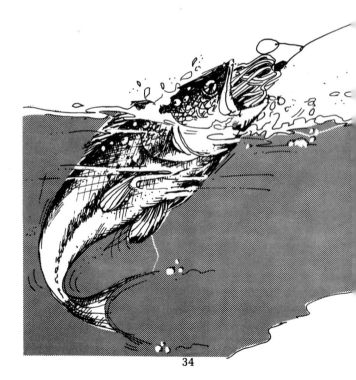

Fish Spinnerbait Skirts With Contrasting Colors

S elect spinnerbait skirts with contrasting colors, such as chartreuse and white, chartreuse and blue, and so on. This color contrast makes the bait more visible in a broader range of water-clarity conditions. A bass initially homes in on a spinner-bait because of the vibrations in the water made by the blade. But when it gets close, an appealing visual appearance may cause the fish to make the final commitment to strike.

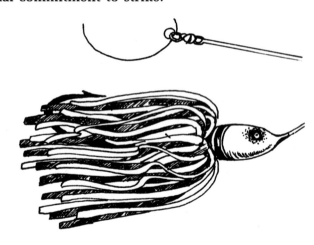

tip 19

Match Spinnerbait Blades To Right Fishing Conditions

S pinnerbait blades come in three basic designs: Colorado, willowleaf, and Indiana. Each design has a specific use. Colorado blades turn slowly and produce the most vibration. Use them in dingy water and in deep-fishing situations. Willowleaf blades spin fast and displace a minimum of water. Use them in current or heavy grass weeds. Indiana blades also turn at high rates of speed; use them in open water when fast retrieves are necessary to provoke strikes.

Indiana Blade

Colorado Blade

Willow-leaf

Use Big Spinnerbaits In Rivers

When using spinnerbaits to work deep cover in rivers, choose large — 1 oz. — single-blade baits. These baits sink fast and stay down in the current. Retrieve the lures fairly fast to keep them off bottom. With practice, you can learn to run these baits just above the bottom and past such bass-holding cover as stumps, brush, rocks, etc.

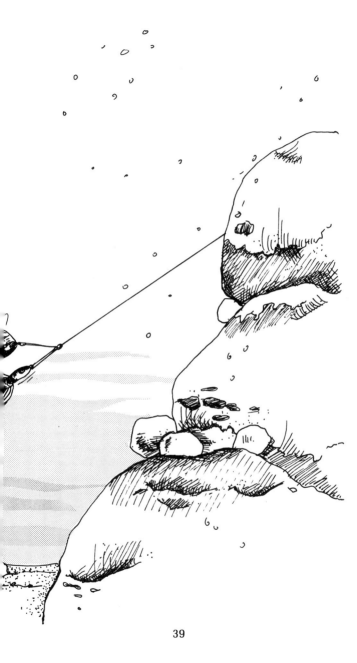

Use Spinnerbaits With Thin-Wire Arms

Spinnerbaits with thin, flexible-wire arms have two advantages over similar lures with stiff-wire arms. As the blade rotates, thin wire bends and pulses with the movement, adding to the spinnerbait's action. Also, when a big bass strikes, often it will inhale the entire bait, not just the skirt and hook. When this happens, heavy wire in a spinnerbait's upper arm may have a weedguard effect and prevent the bass from catching the hook. But a flexible-wire arm will give with the fish's bite and allow the hook to strike home.

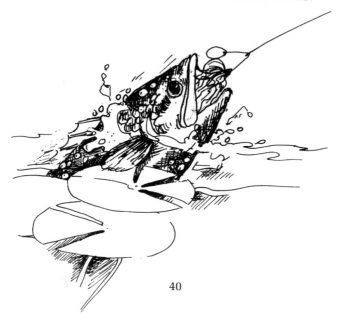

Throw Tandem-Blade
Spinnerbaits In Warm, Clear Water

When fishing spinnerbaits in water that's clear and warm — above 70 degrees — cast tandem-blade models with small or medium blades. In such a situation, a subtle bait with less vibration produces more strikes. The spinning action of the two blades causes each to work against the other. This dampens the vibration and makes the bait more effective than single-blade baits which have more of a throbbing action.

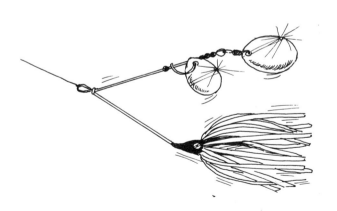

Tie On Plated Spinnerbait
For Greater Visibility

Most spinnerbaits have painted lead heads. But a few baits have heads plated with a gold or nickel finish. Such baits reflect more light and have more flash as they are retrieved. A good rule of thumb is to use gold-plated baits in muddy water and nickel-plated baits in clear water.

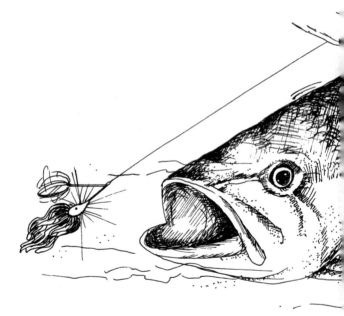

Choose Buzzbait Size According To Water Conditions

Buzzbaits should be chosen by size according to the amount of chop on the water. When the target zone is windswept and choppy, use a larger bait; it makes more noise and disturbance. But when the target zone is calm, a smaller, quieter bait seems to produce more strikes.

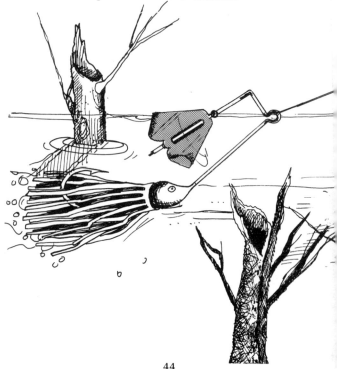

44

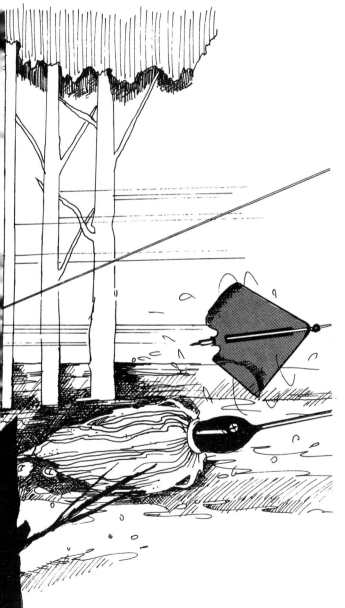

Use Nickel/Gold Spinnerbaits On Surface-Feeding Bass

In deep-summer and under bright sunlight, shad flip to the surface for oxygen. When bass are feeding on these baitfish, use a white tandem-blade spinner with #4 Colorado blades, gold on front and nickel on the back. This color combination resembles baitfish reflected in sunlight. Work your bait with a medium-to-fast retrieve, alternately pulling it just under the surface, then letting it sink a foot before bringing it back near the top.

II

WHERE
TO FISH
SPINNERBAITS

Call Bass Out Of Thick Cover

Sometimes bass can be coaxed out of heavy cover by making a commotion on the surface. Try this technique wherever green vegetation — weeds, lily pads, willow limbs — is too thick to penetrate by normal casting or "crashing."

Use the heaviest spinnerbait in your tacklebox. Slam the bait down onto the water three or four times. Then cast it as close to the cover as possible and allow the lure to sink on a tight line. Sometimes, the racket lures a bass to the edge of the vegetation, where a strike is likely as the bait descends. This method is especially productive in muddy water.

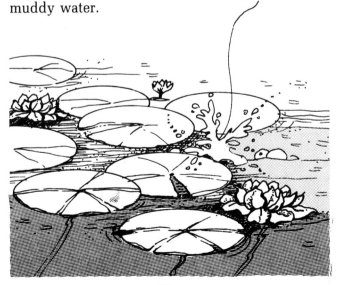

Cast Spinnerbaits Across
Sandbars For River Bass

In rivers, bass often move up onto sandbars adjacent to channels to feed on baitfish. When this situation occurs, employ the cover-a-lot-of-water technique to locate the fish. One way is by holding your boat just off the bar in deep water, working downstream next to the bar, and casting spinnerbaits across the shallows. Use a 1/2-oz. bait with a tandem-rigged Colorado blade backed up by a #8 willowleaf blade. This blade combination throws off a lot of flash and will attract bass from long distances across the flats.

Fish Around Downed Logs With Spinnerbaits

Spinnerbaits are ideal lures to attract bass hiding under downed logs. One of the most productive is a steady retrieve parallel to and very near the log's trunk.

Be thorough and methodical when fishing such structure, working both sides of the log and spots where major branches intersect with the trunk. Let the bait "die" on a tight line after it runs past the end of the log; often a bass will follow the bait to the end of the cover, then pick it off when it starts to drop.

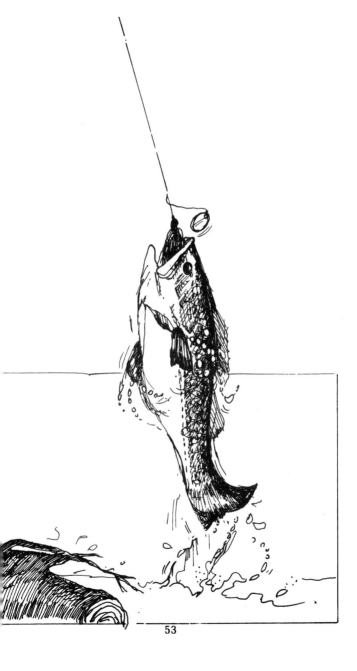

'Crash' Spinnerbait Into Heavy Cover

If bass are holding in heavy brush and can't be enticed out by conventional means, "crashing" the cover may be the only alternative for catching them. This offbeat technique involves heavy baitcasting gear, 30-lb.-test line and a spinnerbait at least 5/8 oz. in weight.

Move in next to the cover. Let out approximately 6 feet of line, and with a quick "around-the-world" swing, crash the bait through the thick stuff. Once it's down in the thicket, flutter it up and down, and be prepared to set the hook quickly.

Select Right Buzzbait For
Thick Weeds

A buzzbait is an excellent choice for fishing in thick vegetation. But you must run it as slowly as possible to allow bass to home-in on the lure. In this circumstance, use tandem-bladed baits or in-line buzzbaits with spoon-shaped bodies. These have greater buoyancy and can ride through the vegetation without snagging. Hence, they can be retrieved slower while still being kept on the surface.

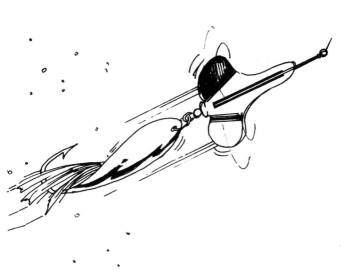

Try Twin-Armed Spinnerbaits In Heavy Cover

To help avoid hang ups in thick cover, use spinnerbaits with twin arms/blades. During retrieve, these arms spread at an angle back over the bait's body and hook, becoming a weedguard. They fend off branches, rocks, and cause the bait to ride over other potential trouble spots without snagging.

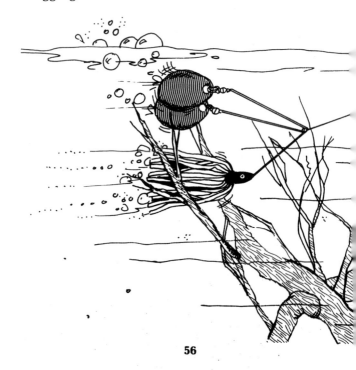

Try 'Ripping' When Bass Are On Deep Structure

When bass are holding on deep structure in clear reservoirs, "ripping" is a good technique for catching them. Cast a 1/2-oz. white single-blade spinnerbait beyond where the fish are holding and allow the lure to flutter to the bottom. Start a slow, steady retrieve, and pull the bait near the target zone. When close to the fish's location, suddenly yank ("rip") the bait forward a foot or two. Then allow the bait to drop straight down. Before it hits bottom, rip it again. Continue this rip/drop retrieve until the bait is well past the target area.

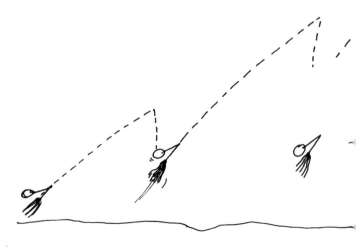

Throw Spinnerbait Along Creek Channels For Early-Season Bass

Prior to spawning, large female bass in reservoirs tend to hold along creek channels leading upstream to spawning areas. To catch these bass, select a medium-sized spinnerbait with a single blade, add a #11 pork chunk, and cast parallel to the creek-channel bank. Allow the bait to settle to the bottom, then slowly crawl it back toward you. Work your way up the creek in this manner, thoroughly fishing areas with stumps or brush.

34 *tip*

Experiment With Retrieve Speeds

Sometimes, bass want a fast-travelling spinner-bait; other times they prefer a slow-moving bait. So start your fishing day with a consciousness of retrieve speed, trying one speed for a while, then switching to another if the bass aren't interested.

After your first strike, duplicate the retrieve speed on succeeding retrieves, at least until you can better determine if speed has any bearing on that day's fishing success.

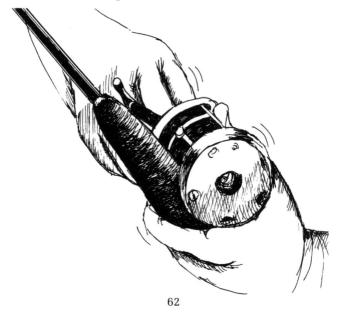

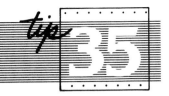

Flutter 'Drop Bait' Beside
Bushes And Stumps

Drop baits are safety-pin spinnerbaits with hinged upper arms. When the lure is stopped in the water, its arm rotates upward and the spinner blade helicopters enticingly during descent.

Fish drop baits around isolated bushes and stumps. Cast past the shady side of the cover and retrieve the bait steadily, just under the surface. As the bait runs past the cover, stop your retrieve, keep the line taut, and let the spinner flutter down. Watch the line, and be prepared to set the hook.

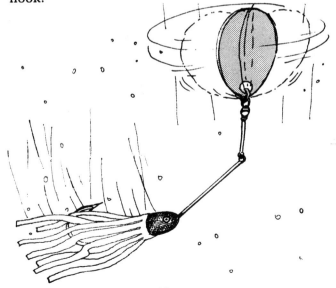

Flip A Spinnerbait

Instead of using plastic worms or jigs when flipping, try a spinnerbait. Swim the bait down logs, bump tree trunks of standing timber, or yo-yo the bait in brush. Sometimes, the throbbing vibration of the blade excites bass holding tight in cover and provokes strikes when conventional flipping baits fail to produce.

'Skip' Spinnerbaits Under Tree Limbs, Boat Docks

Bass sometimes hold underneath boat docks, tree limbs, and other types of overhanging cover. Casting a spinnerbait into these spots is practically impossible — unless you're adept at the "skipping" technique. Use a long spinning rod and matching reel. Cast sidearm, bouncing the bait off the water and skipping it under the cover (like skipping a rock). Begin your retrieve immediately; pull the bait back to the edge of the cover and stop the retrieve, letting the spinnerbait flutter down on a tight line.

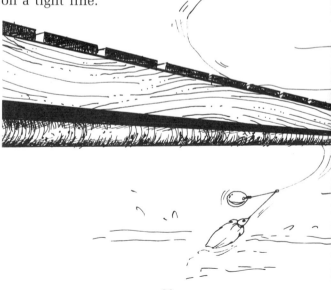

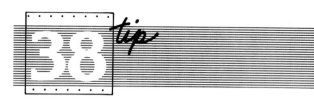

Work All A Grassbed's 'Options'

When bass are in grassbeds, they may be hold-ing in any of several types of spots. Start fishing by buzzing spinners or buzzbaits along the outside edge, parallel to the grassline. If the fish aren't working this outer border, cast into the pockets along this edge. Next, pick out holes in the grass and work them by buzzing or dropping spin-ners into these openings. Finally, if all else fails, try the dense grass itself. Sometimes bass will hole up in such thick stuff, but they will grab a spinner as it runs by.

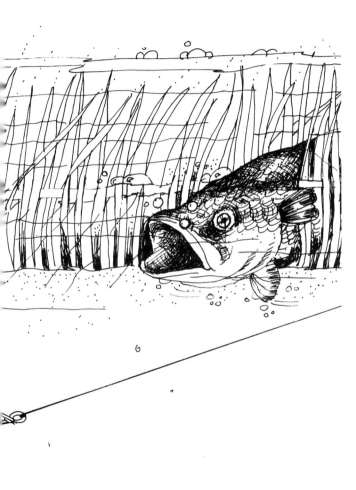

Jig Spinnerbait In Heavy Cover Following Cold Front

Following a severe cold front, bass may concentrate in deep brushpiles or stumps and become finicky feeders. In such a situation, ease your boat directly over the timber and with your reel in freespool, drop a spinnerbait straight down into the cover. After the lure settles on bottom, engage the spool, lift the bait a foot to 18 inches, then let it flutter back down. Continue to work the cover patiently and thoroughly, and always be ready for that slight tap or unnatural tension which might indicate a strike.

12 inches

Use 'Weed Walker' In
Super-Thick Vegetation

Fishing a spinnerbait or buzzbait in extremely thick vegetation such as milfoil, moss, or lily pads often results in the bait becoming fouled. But the "Weed Walker" buzzbait is designed just for this type cover. A flat planing body holds a paddlewheel spinner, making the bait a cross between a spoon and a buzzer. It's deadly at catching big bass lurking beneath a jungle of vegetation.

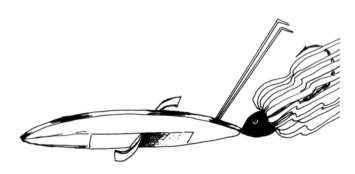

Use Big Spinnerbait Along Mud Line

Following a hard rain, a mud line may form in a reservoir and move slowly downstream. Many times, bass stack up just ahead of such a line, concentrating in the clear water as the muddy water advances. When a distinct mud line can be seen, cast a large, brightly colored spinnerbait into the muddy water. As it reaches the clear zone, slow your retrieve so the bait begins a controlled drop. Be ready for a strike just as the lure exits from the mud line.

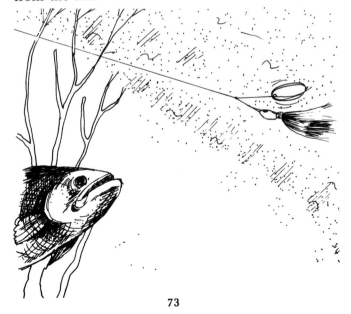

Cast Buzzbait Several Times To 'High-Probability' Spot

By making repeated casts to a productive-looking area, you frequently can induce an active bass to strike your buzzbait. Try this technique when fishing isolated brushpiles, treetops, stumps, and similar structure. As many as 10 to 15 casts to the same spot may have an infuriating effect on a reluctant fish, ultimately resulting in an enraged strike.

74

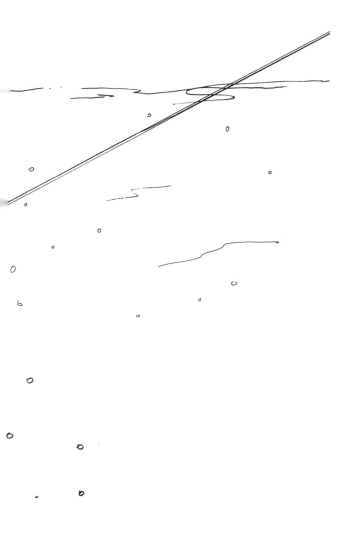

Work Deep Structure At Night For Summer Bass

An effective technique for taking summer bass from clear lakes is to work spinnerbaits along deep structure at night. Concentrate on likely spots such as roadbeds, islands, and sloping points in 20-30 feet of water. Use a 1/2- or 5/8-oz. bait with a single #4 Colorado blade. Allow the bait to sink to the bottom, then retrieve it close to the structure. "Feel" for the bottom three to four times during the retrieve by allowing the spinnerbait to fall. Most strikes occur as the lure is picked back up from the bottom.

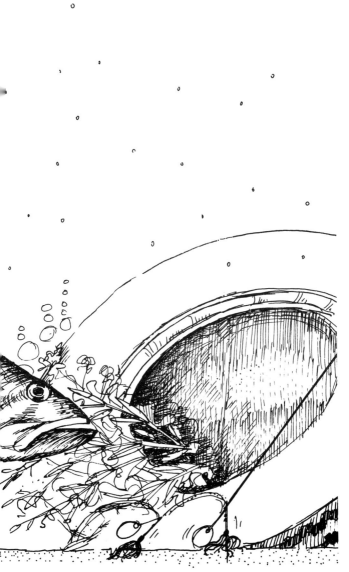

Try Hesitation Retrieve Around Cover

When retrieving a spinnerbait past submerged cover, slow your retrieve so the bait begins to sink slowly. Make sure, however, to keep the lure moving forward on a tight line so it remains in an upright position. Such a retrieve imitates baitfish swimming down to investigate the cover, and this natural movement is tempting to bass lurking nearby.

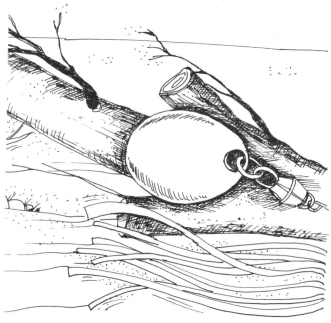

After Dark, Cast Buzzbait Along Riprap Banks

During summertime, bass may stay deep in the day and come up at night to feed. One good place to find them after dark is along riprap banks, and a good way to catch them is casting buzzbaits just off the rocks.

Hold your boat close to the riprap and work parallel to the bank. Use a treble trailer hook, and regardless of the splash a striking fish makes, hesitate momentarily before setting the hook. It's a good idea, too, to wear clear, protective eyeglasses in such a situation.

Use Buzzbait's 'Veer' To Fish Under Limbs, Piers

Single-blade buzzbaits have a built-in torque, resulting in tendency to veer to one direction or another. You can put this trait to good use by casting close to low limbs, boat docks, or similar types of overhanging cover, then allowing the torque to run the bait under this cover to previously unreachable bass.

III

SPINNERBAIT
TIPS
AND TACKLE

Cast Spinnerbaits With Stout Rod

The most popular rod for fishing spinnerbaits is the 5 1/2', medium-action baitcasting rod. Many pros, however, use heavy-action, 6' rods when tossing spinners. The extra length allows more line to be taken up during the hookset, and that, combined with the rod's heavy action, provides better striking power.

Use Black Lights When Working Spinnerbaits At Night

When night fishing for bass with spinnerbaits, use black light illumination and fluorescent monofilament line. In the black light the mono glows, and any unnatural twitches or movements are easily seen, even while the lure is falling on a slack line.

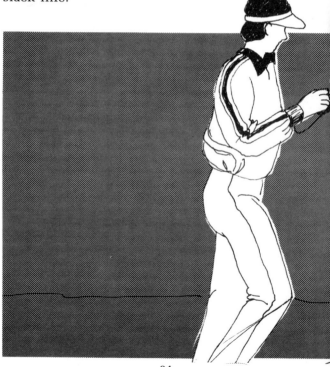

Buzz Spinnerbait With Long Rod

Buzzing a spinnerbait just under the water's surface is a proven way to take shallow bass. And buzzing is easier to do if you use a rod about 7' in length. The long rod gives a higher retrieve angle, moving the bait to the surface faster and holding it there easier. Also, such a rod gives more hook-setting leverage when a strike occurs.

Match Line Size
To Fishing Depth, Cover

When fishing with spinnerbaits, match line size to water depth and the predominant type of cover. In shallow water (surface to 6 feet) and in heavy cover (grass, brush, treetops), use 14- to 17-lb.-test line. When working deeper, cleaner structure, opt for lighter line in the 8- to 12-lb.-test range. Lighter line offers better sensitivity when baits are deep, and it allows you to better feel subtle strikes.

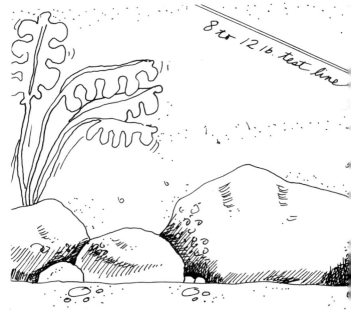

8 to 12 lb. test line

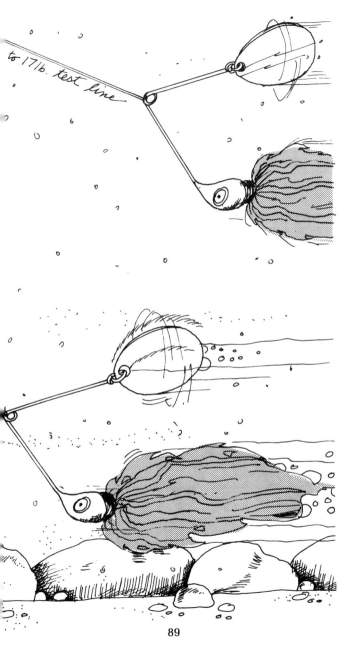

89

Back Up Buzzbait With Spinnerbait

When casting a buzzbait, keep a spinnerbait of the same color rigged on a backup rod. If a bass rolls at a buzzbait but doesn't take it, make a quick followup cast with the spinnerbait. Sometimes an aggravated fish which won't commit to the surface bait will show no hesitation to strike a similar bait offered below the surface.

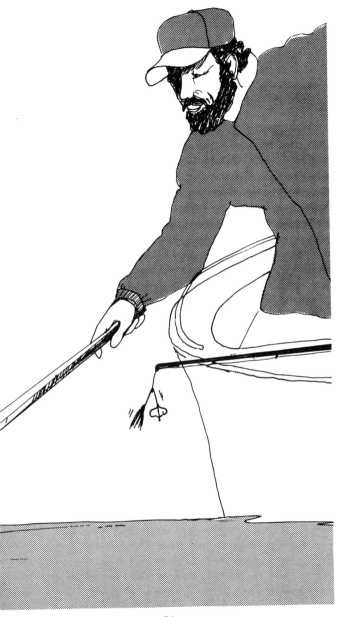

Vertical-Jig Spinnerbait Next To Standing Cover

S uspended bass have an affinity for such verti-cal structure as tree trunks, bridge pilings, and rock ledges. Take advantage of this — if the water is deep enough — by quietly positioning your boat next to the structure, then jigging your spinnerbait up and down beside the timber or ledge. Allow the bait to flutter down on a free-spool, being ready to strike if you notice a twitch of your line. Jig the bait at different depths to cover all possible ranges in which bass could be holding.

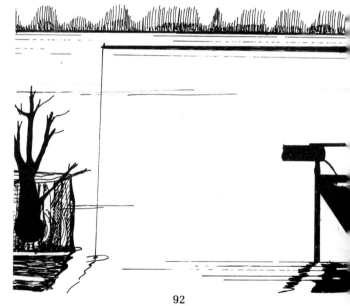

53 *tip*

React Fast When Bass Strike

Strikes on spinnerbaits come fast, and a fish quickly detects that its prey isn't a natural food. So stay alert, keep your line tight and be ready to set the hook immediately when you feel a bite or see your line move unnaturally.

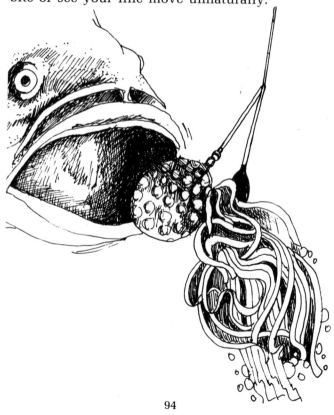

Use Currents To Carry Spinnerbaits To Bass

In currents, feeding bass often hold under such cover as bushes, trees, limbs, and logjams, waiting for food to wash to them. In this situation, hold your boat cross-current from the cover. Cast a lightweight spinnerbait just upstream and beyond it and retrieve the bait to the upstream edge of the cover. Then stop the retrieve and allow the current to wash the bait under the cover. When the bait should be close to the fish, restart the retrieve. Strikes are likely both when the bait is washing in and being pulled back out from the cover.

Work Spinnerbaits In Shallow Water When Water Temperature Is High

In extremely hot weather, when water temperature nears or exceeds 90 degrees, the oxygen level in a body of water is very shallow and near the surface. When this condition prevails, concentrate on working the first 2 feet of water, casting spinnerbaits into thick vegetation or beside logs, stumps and other types of cover which could provide bass some shady relief from the sun's heat.

'Skitter' Spinnerbait To Simulate Baitfish Action

Spinnerbaits retrieved just under the surface create a rippling trail, a proven attractor of big bass. To give such a retrieve added attraction, occasionally pull the bait faster so the blade breaks the water's surface. This "skittering" action looks like a panic-stricken baitfish trying to flee a predator. This often will incite bass to attack the lure.

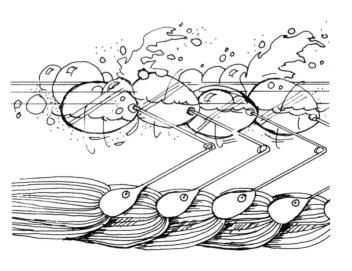

Hesitate Momentarily On Buzzbait Strike

Bass sometimes have trouble making good contact with a buzzbait, especially in heavy cover. Thus, if you strike too fast you pull the bait away and miss a hookup. So instead of setting the hook instantly, hesitate a split second to either feel the fish or to see that the bait has disappeared below the surface. If the bass missed the bait, continue a steady retrieve, and chances are the fish will strike again.

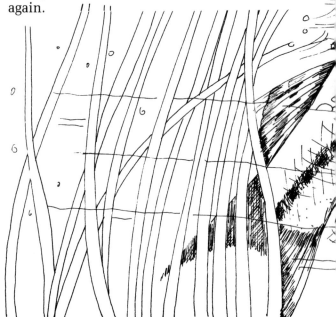

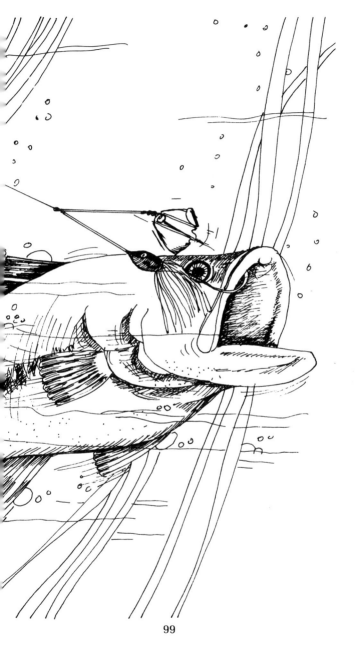

Retrieve Spinnerbaits Just Below Visibility Level

When fishing around cover in stained water, retrieve a spinnerbait just below the visibility level — the depth at which the bait disappears from your sight. If, for example, the bait disappears when lowered 12 inches into the water, fish at a depth of about 14 inches. Generally, this is where most bass will be holding, meaning that your spinnerbait will probably produce best at this level.

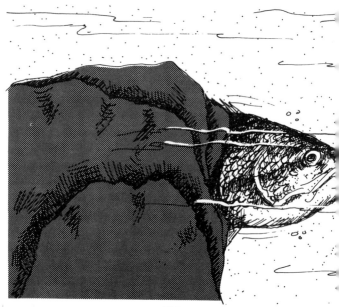

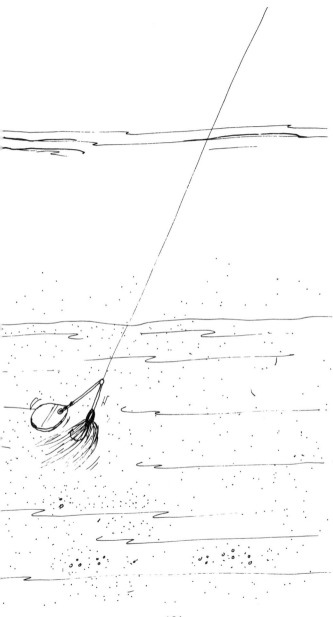

Alter Retrieve Depth According To Sunlight Conditions

Use the amount of sunlight to judge how and where to fish spinnerbaits. On bright, sunny days, bass stay deeper or in shady cover. In this case retrieve the bait deeper, and cast into shady areas (spring and summer). On cloudy, rainy days, the bass hold away from cover, so retrieve spinners at or near the surface. Move in close to the target area, and make short, accurate casts.

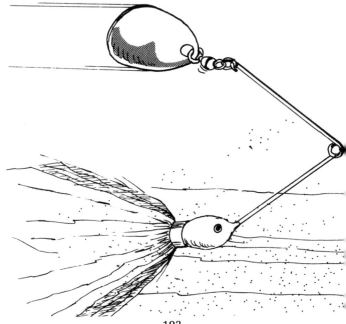

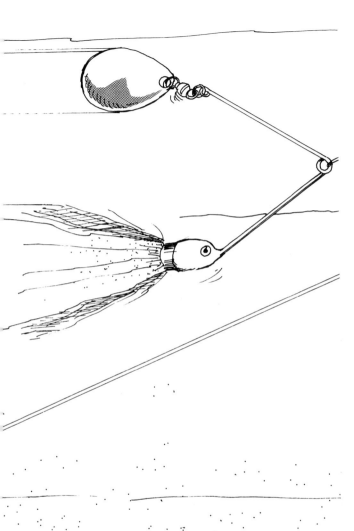

Use 'Two-Rod' Approach
When Fishing Spinnerbaits

When casting spinnerbaits around shallow cover, it's a good idea to rig two rods: one with a tandem-blade, larger bait, and a second with a smaller, single-blade bait of the same color. If a bass swirls at, but turns down, the larger bait, make another quick cast with the second rod and smaller lure. Sometimes this second spinnerbait with a more subtle action will be the right enticement to cause a strike.

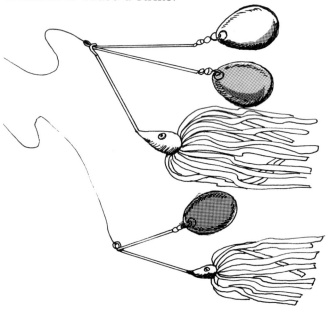

Avoid 'Jerking' Spinnerbait In Heavy Cover

Spinnerbaits are semi-weedless by design, and various models have additional weedguards to make them even less likely to hang. But they can still snag, especially if you don't retrieve them properly — if, for instance, you jerk the bait when it runs onto cover. To ensure against hang ups, maintain a normal retrieve speed up to the cover, then slow the bait down, and crawl it through the limbs or weeds.

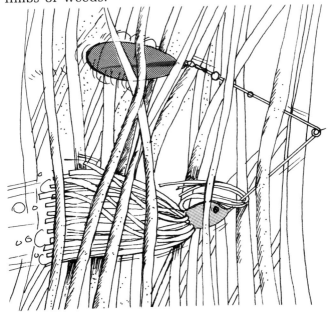

Stop Buzzbait Before It Contacts Water

After hitting the water, a buzzbait sinks immediately, requiring you to reel quickly the first few feet to pull it back to the surface. This initial sinking can be avoided, however, by stopping the cast while the lure is in midair, then starting the retrieve just before the bait touches the water.

Catch Following Bass With Stop-Go Retrieve

Often, a bass will follow a spinnerbait back to the boat, striking just as the bait is lifted from the water. To solidly hook more of these following fish, try this technique: After working the primary strike zone — stump, rocks, edge of grassbed — retrieve the lure steadily back toward the boat. Halfway in, stop the bait, let it fall momentarily, then resume a fast retrieve. Many times this will provoke following fish to strike while there's still enough line out to hook and play the fish properly.

64 *tip*

Maintain Tight-Line Contact On Falling Spinnerbait

S pinnerbaits are effective on bass in deep structure. For best results, pump the lures off bottom and let them flutter back down. When the bait is falling — after the cast or during retrieve — maintain contact with the lure by having at least a moderately tight line. Otherwise your spinnerbait will cartwheel, and you'll miss subtle strikes.

Avoid Using Snaps Or Swivels With Spinnerbaits

Spinnerbaits are designed to be tied directly to the line, without a snap or swivel. Addition of either increases the chance that the bait will roll over, producing ineffective retrieve and line twist. So don't use these tackle items when fishing with spinnerbaits or buzzbaits.

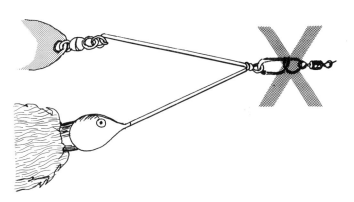

Experiment With Spinnerbait Retrieves

O n any given day bass may prefer one style retrieve to another. So experiment to find what works best. The steady pull is a good starting place, but a good alternative is the stop-pull-stop retrieve. Each time the bait is stopped, the skirt billows out, and sometimes this seems to cause strikes from fish which would otherwise just watch a steady-swimming spinnerbait.

Work Spinnerbaits With Graphite Or Boron Rods

High-content graphite or graphite/boron casting rods are more suited to working spinnerbaits than are fiberglass rods, agree many pros. Graphite and boron material in rods make them more sensitive to subtle strikes; too, these rods also are "faster," meaning the hook-setting power transfers from the angler's hands to the rod tip more quickly than with fiberglass rods. This faster hookset translates into more "stuck" fish per number of strikes.

Give Bass A Second Chance

When a bass "short-strikes" a spinnerbait, stop the bait in the water, let it fall, rip it a short distance and then let it fall again. This may convince the fish that he's crippled his prey, and he will attack again for the easy kill.

'Crawl' Spinners In Early Spring

In early spring, when water temperatures are below 65 degrees, retrieve spinners at a slow crawl, barely fast enough to keep them off bottom. In colder water, the bass' metabolism is slower, and the fish are more likely to strike a slow-moving, near-the-bottom bait. Keep the retrieve steady and straight. If anything alters the blade's rpm pattern, think "strike" and set the hook.

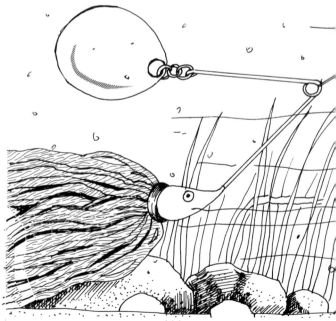

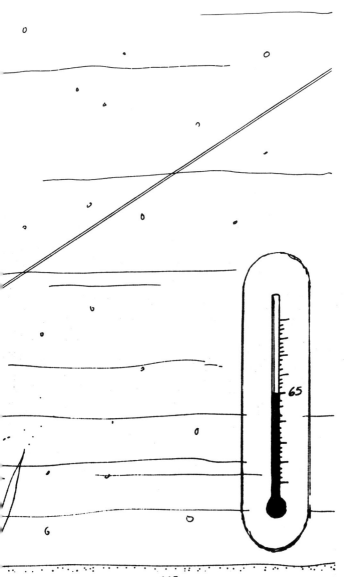

115

Use 'Long-Pole, Buzzing' Method On Inactive Bass

When bass are holding in shallow cover and aren't actively feeding, sometimes they still can be caught via the "long-pole, buzzing" method. This technique involves a 12-foot, stiff fiberglass pole, 40-pound monofilament line and a buzzbait. Use only 2 feet of line, and swim the bait in, around and through likely cover. Work the bait slowly and thoroughly in tight spots which can't be reached by normal casting. When a bass strikes, set the hook and immediately swing the fish into the boat.

IV

ALTERING SPINNERBAITS

Add Extra Weight
To Spinnerbait

Adding extra weight to a spinnerbait allows a longer cast and a truer retrieve. Split-shot sinkers may be used to increase heft, but a better option is an oval-shaped, rubber-core sinker. Remove the rubber and clamp the sinker onto the wire just ahead of the leadhead.

Add Pork Chunk For More Buoyancy

The best way to hold a rod while retrieving a spinnerbait is at an angle pointed toward where the line enters the water. Such a position allows for a taut line and a fast, lifting hookset when a strike comes. But when fishing shallow water, oftentimes it's difficult to hold the rod in this position and still keep the bait off bottom as it's riding in. This problem can be alleviated by adding a large pork chunk (#1 size) as a trailer. The pork gives the bait buoyancy and causes it to stay up in the water.

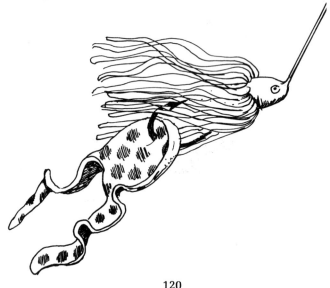

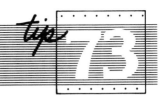

Change Spinner Blades
When Necessary

Different sizes or shapes of spinner blades may be alternated on the same bait to match varying fishing conditions. For buzzing or retrieving just under the surface, replace the standard-sized blade with an oversized blade (#7 or #8). In extremely clear or deep water, downsize the blade to a #4. If baitfish are small, changing to a willow-leaf blade might produce more strikes. Buy extra spinner blades in a variety of shapes and sizes, and store them in a plastic bag in your tacklebox for on-the-spot modifications.

74 tip

'Spread Arms' To Fish Spinnerbait Slowly

When bass aren't actively feeding, try slowing your spinnerbait's retrieve speed. If, however, this leads to problems with the blade(s) not turning properly, bend the wire arms apart. The blades will then spin freely. Reminder: After this alteration is made, don't attempt to retrieve your spinnerbait at high speed. To do so will cause the lure to "windmill."

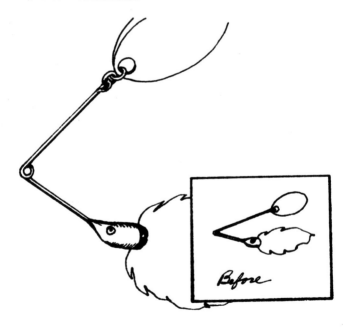

Before

Tune Spinnerbait For Correct Alignment

For a spinnerbait to run as straight and as weedless as possible, the bait's upper arm should be aligned with the shank of the hook. Baits that begin to snag frequently should be checked for arm alignment, and adjustments (corrective bends) should be made accordingly. This is called "tuning the spinnerbait."

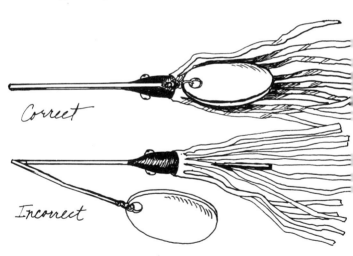

Correct

Incorrect

Fish Spinnerbait With Large Blades For Larger Bass

B ass tend to school according to size. Big bass seem to stay with other big fish; small bass typically congregate with their own size.

If you locate a concentration of large bass, tempt them with a spinnerbait having a large blade. A #6 or #7 blade gives the bait more sound and flash, and it looks like bigger food.

Use Powder On Spinnerbait Skirts

Rubber skirts are popular on spinnerbaits because of their lifelike action. But hot weather can cause your supply of replacement skirts to stick together or to your tacklebox. A good way to avoid this problem is to store skirts in a plastic bag containing a small amount of baby powder. Doing this ensures that the dressings will remain soft, dry, and stick-free.

Alter Skirt For Better Action, Hook-Setting

Reversing a spinnerbait's skirt causes it to billow, offering a fluttering, more enticing action as the lure runs through the water. Also, trimming the skirt to no more than 1/4-inch longer than the outside curve of the hook increases the odds of hooking a short-striking bass.

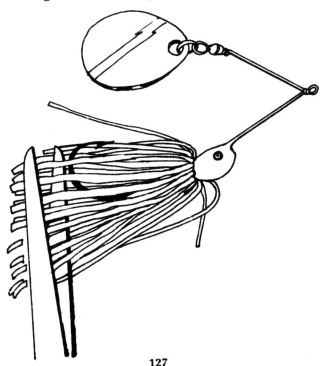

Sharpen Spinnerbait Hooks

Sharp hooks catch more bass, whether they're on spinnerbaits, crankbaits, or any other lure. The best hook sharpener is a flat file, and the best sharpening technique is to file the point in triangular fashion (on three different sides). Sharpening via this method creates three cutting edges running up to the point (like a pyramid) which can slice their way into a bass' bony mouth tissue.

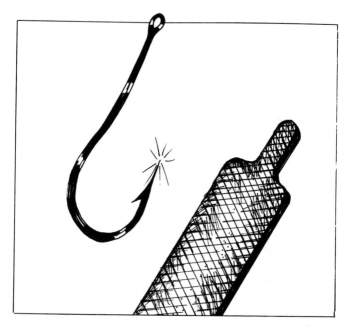

Carve Barb Onto
Spinnerbait Collar

Most lead heads on spinnerbaits have a collar to hold the skirt in place. If a problem arises with the skirt continually slipping down over the hook, carve a barb in the soft collar with a pocket-knife. This will snag the skirt and keep it snug up against the head of the bait.

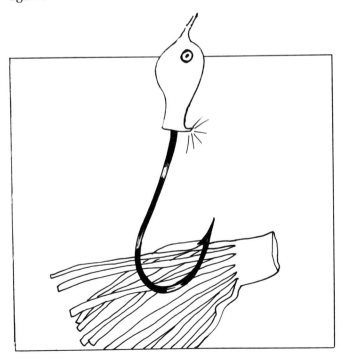

Perform Annual Checkup On Spinnerbaits

Prior to each fishing season, inspect spinner-baits and repair any damages. If lead heads are roughed up or missing paint, remove the skirt, file the head smooth (being careful not to alter the basic shape) and repaint with automotive paint. When the head dries, replace the old skirt with a new one. Polish blades with an abrasive cleaner. Finally, resharpen the hook to a keen point. When this overhaul is completed, the bait will resemble a new one, and it'll be ready for a new year.

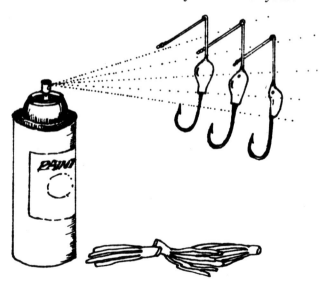

Add 'Texas-Style' Worm To
Make Spinnerbait Weedless

Semi-weedless by design, spinnerbaits still hang up in heavy cover. One way to greatly increase their weedlessness is to use a plastic worm as a trailer, rigging the worm Texas-style on the bait's hook (running the hook point through the worm's head, sliding the worm up the shank and then turning the hook around and burying the barb back in the worm). When fishing a spinnerbait rigged in this manner, extra strength is required in the hookset when a strike is detected.

Try Crawfish Trailers On Spinnerbaits

When fishing in locations and at times of year when bass should be feeding on crawfish, use plastic crawfish trailers on the back of spinnerbaits. Add this trailer behind the skirt, or remove the skirt and use only the plastic trailer. Regardless of the configuration, retrieve this lure slowly and close to the bottom.

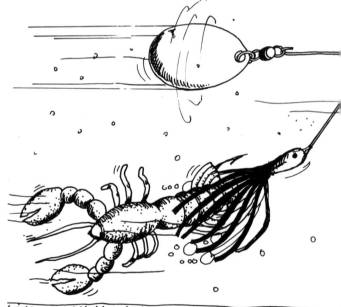

Use Rubber Band To Ensure Against Snagging

Rig a small rubber band on your spinnerbait to reduce hang ups. Loop the rubber band through the eye of the bait, stretch it back, and hook it under the barb of the hook. The rubber guard will repel limbs or grass, but it will give way and bare the hook when a bass strikes.

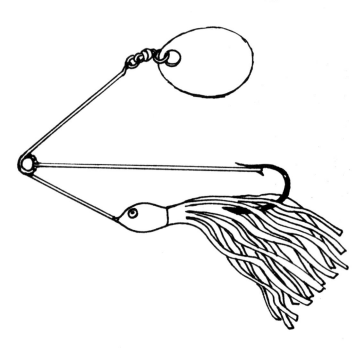

Spray Spinnerbait Skirts With 'Scotch Guard' To Prevent Sticking

Rubber skirts stick together when stored in warm, moist places, such as a plastic bag or a tacklebox. One way to prevent this sticking is by spraying Scotch Guard or a similar silicon lubricant on the skirts before storing them; the silicon spray keeps the skirts supple and fresh for long periods.

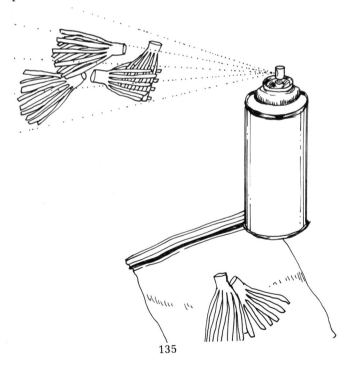

At Night, Keep Your Retrieve Steady

When night fishing with spinnerbaits, use a steady retrieve instead of an erratic one. The steady vibrations help guide a bass to your lure; an erratic, jerky retrieve, however, may cause the fish to have difficulty homing in on the bait.

Change Blades For Hesitant Bass

If bass are reluctant to strike your spinnerbait, changing the blade style and size may make the lure more enticing to the fish. Replacing Colorado-style blades with smaller Indiana-style blades causes a more subtle, less noisy action that may turn a bland day on the water into a terrific one.

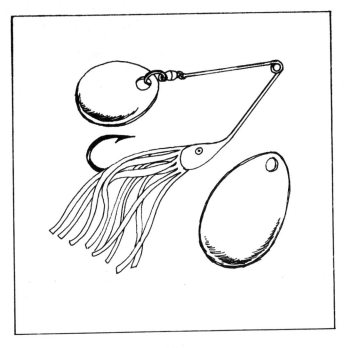

Retrieve Spinnerbait Slowly In Cold Water

Worked slowly, spinnerbaits can be very effective when the water temperature is below 60 degrees, making bass sluggish. When fishing under such conditions, keep your rod tip low to the water; this provides more striking leverage when you detect a hit. Also add a #1 pork chunk to your bait for more buoyancy and to help keep the lure off bottom during a slow retrieve.

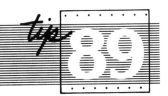

Use Treble Hook Trailer
On Buzzbait

Buzzbaits are good lures for random-casting at surface-feeding bass. When fishing open water — clear shorelines, points, beside docks — a treble-hook trailer is effective on short-striking bass. A treble hook doesn't interfere with the bait's action, and it vastly increases your chances for a good hookset.

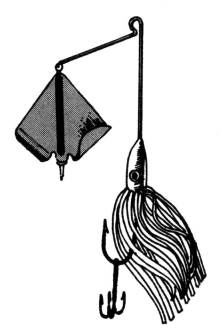

Thin Spinnerbait Skirts For Better Action

Many spinnerbaits are sold with skirts too thick to provide the proper freedom of movement. The best action comes from skirts with a small number — 18 to 20 — of rubber strands. Once thinned down, these skirts should always be reversed before being positioned on the hook. This combination of thinning and reversal gives maximum billowing and flowing of the skirt as the bait is pulled through the water.

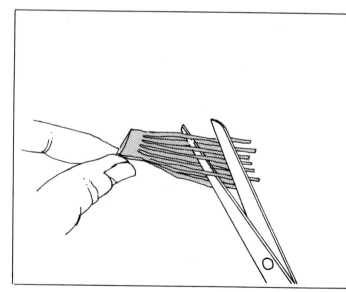

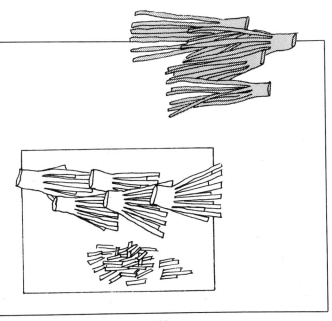

Spool On Braided Dacron Line For Long-Distance Casting

When making long, searching casts with a buzzbait or spinnerbait, use braided dacron line instead of monofilament. Long lengths of most types of monofilament have a certain amount of stretch when the hook is set — but not braided dacron. This translates into more shock power in the hookset at longer distances. So you won't have to change line frequently, keep an extra reel spooled with braided dacron in your tacklebox and just swap reels when necessary.

Alter A Buzzbait's
Retrieve Speed

Most buzzbait strikes occur when the bait is pulled at a steady pace. Sometimes, however, jerking the bait, creating a commotion on the surface, produces strikes by stubborn bass. Following bass probably think that when the bait speeds up and makes extra noise, it's either trying to escape, or another fish is attacking it. In either case, the abrupt change in retrieve may excite such fish into striking. Usually this technique is used after a buzzbait is pulled past the target cover and is headed back to the boat.

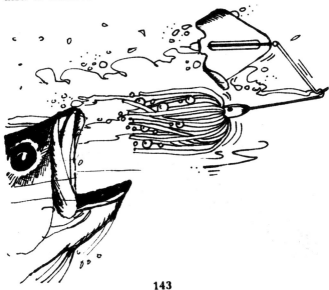

Bend Buzzbait Arm To Make More Racket

In many cases, the buzzbaits that make the most noise provoke the most strikes. Because of this, many anglers bend the upper arm of a buzzbait down, so the blade barely hits the lower arm as it rotates. If positioned properly, the blade still turns freely, but as it rotates, it gives off a "clack, clack, clack" sound during retrieve.

Make Your Own Spinnerbaits

Create custom-made spinnerbaits from parts ordered from mail-order houses. Several tackle-crafting companies offer molds, hooks, wire, spinner blades, and other essential parts for assembling baits to meet specific desires or designs. In this way, you can do it yourself and come up with exactly the lure you need for a special fishing situation.

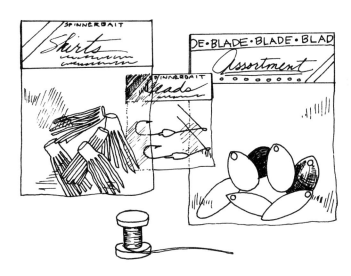

Always Consider Boat Position
When Casting Spinnerbaits

One difference between average spinnerbait users and the experts is attention to boat position when working a target area. The experts always pay close attention to proper position. They visualize where bass should be in relation to the target, and they position their boat for greatest casting advantage to that particular spot. The ideal situation is to be able to cast beyond the target zone and to retrieve the lure along visual structure's "grain" — beside a log, the same direction limbs are growing in treetops, brushpiles, and so forth.

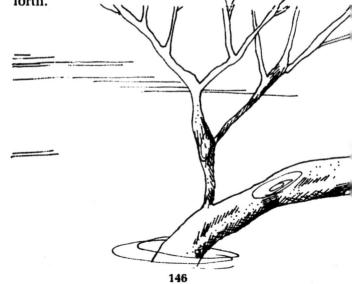

Drill Holes In Spinnerbait Blades For More Noise, Commotion

Small holes in the center of a spinnerbait's blades create more noise and air bubbles as the lure is retrieved, often translating into more strikes. Use an electric drill to drill the holes, but be careful not to tear or twist the blade.

Air-Test Buzzbait After Tuning

For a buzzbait to run at maximum efficiency, its spinner blade must turn freely. Experiment with tuning by bending the blade to different angles. Then test its ease-of-turn by blowing on the blade from the front of the bait. The bait is properly tuned when the blade turns freely at the slightest breath of air.

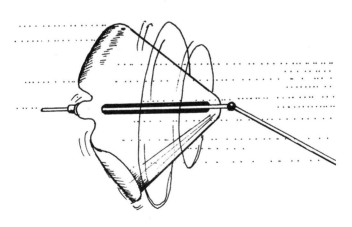

149

Use Fish Attractants On Spinnerbaits

Fish attractant formulas are proven producers, especially when fishing is slow. Chemical attractants can sometimes spur non-feeding bass into a feeding mood.

Periodically douse your spinnerbait's skirt with your choice of attractant. Then cast several times to the same high-potential spot. As the bait's scent trail disperses through the water, it may provoke an inactive fish into striking.

Bend Tandem Buzzbait's Front Blade For More Noise

When using a tandem-blade buzzbait, bend the cups on the front blade backward so they nick the rear blade when they turn. This contact creates a noisy commotion during the retrieve. This noise irritates bass and sometimes causes reluctant fish to strike.

Attach Trailer Hook For Better Hook-Setting

Trailer hooks are a good idea when bass are short-striking spinnerbaits. Put the eye of the trailer over the point of the spinnerbait's hook, then down onto its bend. Secure it by adding some type of hook keeper (a piece of plastic, surgical tubing, etc.) onto the spinner hook between its barb and the trailer. This lodges against the barb and keeps the trailer hook from slipping back off the spinner hook.

Trailer hooks are very effective except in heavy cover, when they cause problems by fouling on grass, brush, etc. Trial-and-error will teach you when and where not to use a trailer.

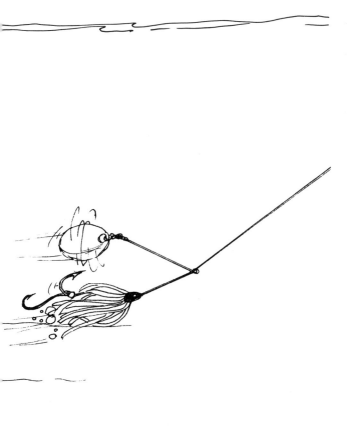

NOTES

NOTES

NOTES

NOTES

NOTES

NOTES

NOTES